GOOD · OLD · DAYS

Live It Again™

1943

Dear Friends,

Freedom of want. Freedom of speech. Freedom of worship. Freedom of fear.

No four slogans better epitomized what we were fighting for as 1943 unfolded. And no American artist could illustrate them better than Norman Rockwell. In 1941, Rockwell heard a speech by President Franklin D. Roosevelt that inspired him to paint *The Four Freedoms*, published in February and March 1943 issues of *The Saturday Evening Post*.

Rockwell had long captured the heart and soul of America on canvas. In more than 50 years he painted 323 covers for the *Post*. In 1943 alone he painted five covers in addition to *The Four Freedoms*.

It was Rockwell who introduced America to *Rosie the Riveter* on May 29, 1943. Rosie became so associated with strong American women taking the place of courageous fighting men that Rockwell repeated the theme with *Rosie to the Rescue* in the *Post's* Sept. 4 issue (featured on the cover of this wonderful book). This time Rosie was clothed in Old Glory and rushing headlong into nursing, gardening, delivering milk and working the factories—all of the inglorious jobs that kept the Allied forces focused on defeating the Axis powers in World War II.

> **Rockwell had long captured the heart and soul of America on canvas.**

In this powerful yearbook dedicated to the momentous and mundane events that made up 1943, we spotlight the career of Norman Rockwell as he became America's most beloved artist. We also highlight the work of women both on the home front and in frontline hospitals.

We also capture the fun, romance, laughter and tears that made every day a joy and a challenge as we fought for The Four Freedoms in 1943.

Contents

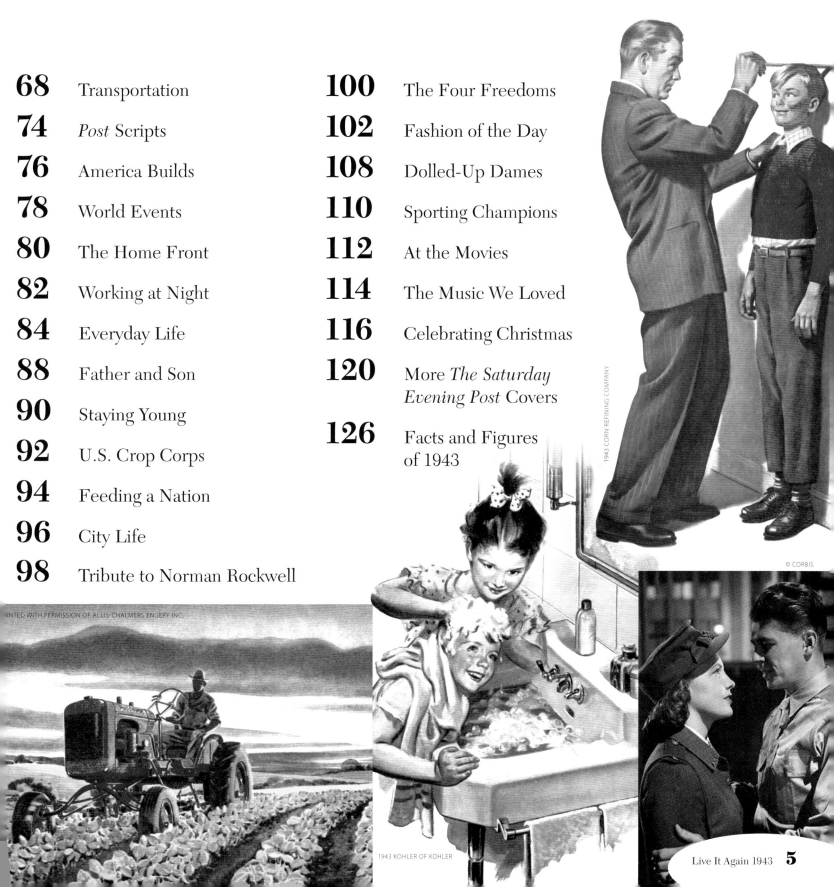

1943 CORN REFINING COMPANY

© CORBIS

PRINTED WITH PERMISSION OF ALLIS-CHALMERS ENGERY INC.

1943 KOHLER OF KOHLER

Victory Gardens

A scene that had previously been familiar on rural farms sprung up in urban areas during the war as metropolitan America answered the call to plant "Victory Gardens." An estimated 20 million Americans planted vegetable and flower spreads in backyards, empty lots and on rooftops in order to supplement certain foods that were hard to get due to rationing.

Products such as sugar, butter, milk, cheese, eggs, meat and canned goods were rationed as part of the war effort. In addition, it proved difficult to move fruits and vegetables to market because of gas being rationed.

During World War II government leaders turned to Americans to provide at least a portion of their own truck foods. Residents of the United Kingdom and Canada also participated in the effort. At selective sites, such as Boston's Fenway Victory Gardens and the Dowling Community Garden in Minneapolis, efforts remain active as an example of the World War II effort.

1943 MOTOR BUS LINES OF AMERICA

Americans took pride in connecting their gardening efforts with the war involvement of military serving on the battlefield.

FAMOUS BIRTHDAYS
Janis Joplin, January 19
Rock singer
Princess Margriet, January 19
Of the Netherlands

...ONWARD *Garden* SOLDIERS!

many plots, merican flags or ositive slogans dicated support for e military effort of orld War II.

© LIBRARY OF CONGRESS, PRINTS AND PHOTOGRAPHS DIVISION, CPH 3B17339

Proud families posed with pride at the success of their community effort in growing vegetables to help sustain the food chain during World War II.

Rationing

Everyone helps

Due to fuel and product demand during the war, the United States government developed a rationing plan which limited usage of gas, food and other essentials for war production. In order to implement the program, ration books containing stamps were issued to assist in these purchases. The books limited purchases over a certain period of time. Foods rationed included sugar, milk, eggs, meat and other types of edible products.

Distribution lines for ration books were often long and confusing. Instructions concerning usage specified that it was unlawful to sell stamps to any other person. Violation resulted in up to a $10,000 fine and possible imprisonment. Still, theft of stamps was a primary crime activity during the time. The story of one couple whose stamps were stolen on their honeymoon was typical of the times. Relatives pooled stamps together and delivered them to the newly-married couple so they could drive their vehicle home.

The government descriptions of rationing regulations were often very complicated and took plenty of study.

© LIBRARY OF CONGRESS, PRINTS AND PHOTOGRAPHS DIVISION, FSA-8E10785

War ration books containing a certain number of stamps were distributed to regulate the sale of gasoline in order to reserve its usage for war vehicle consumption.

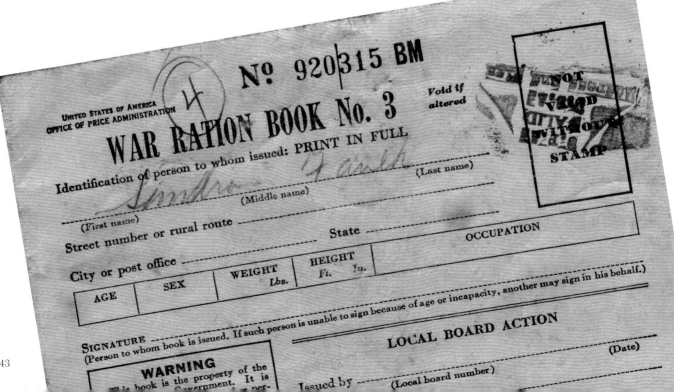

UNITED STATES OF AMERICA
OFFICE OF PRICE ADMINISTRATION

No. 920315 BM

WAR RATION BOOK No. 3

Void if altered

Identification of person to whom issued: PRINT IN FULL

(First name) _____ (Middle name) _____ (Last name)

Street number or rural route _____

City or post office _____ State _____ OCCUPATION

| AGE | SEX | WEIGHT Lbs. | HEIGHT Ft. In. | |

NOT VALID WITHOUT STAMP

SIGNATURE _____ (Person to whom book is issued. If such person is unable to sign because of age or incapacity, another may sign in his behalf.)

LOCAL BOARD ACTION

Issued by _____ (Local board number) _____ (Date)

WARNING This book is the property of the Government. It is

Americans often waited in line for hours in order to obtain the ration stamps to purchase enough gas for travel back and forth to work and to buy essential items.

© 1943 SEPS

"And in the end they found their ration books, and lived happily ever after."

Putting stamps in ration books was a way of including children, giving them a sense of being involved in war sacrifices.

Many Americans made their own clothes, grew their own vegetables and became self-sufficient in other areas in order to meet family needs that would otherwise by rationed.

A punctured tire was a major crisis due to the shortage of rubber and the difficulty in replacing the tire during ration times. Tire repair kits were a common necessity of home supplies.

"What have you got for two points that goes well with mustard greens?"

Rationing

Making it work

American citizens were asked to help with the rationing of approximately 20 items so that these various products derived from rationing could be shipped to troops for war supplies. Items such as metal, rubber, fabrics, gasoline, liquor and canned goods were needed for war supply support.

Very quickly, a black market developed in both rationed goods and phony ration books. By 1943, War Ration Book Two was issued with a point system designed to stop much of the illegal activity. Points were assigned to certain goods with a specific number allowed to each person for a year's time.

The points practice gave teeth to the rationing principle and allowed the Office of Price Administration to control the distribution of sales and prevent acute shortages and high inflation.

Recipes were modified to accommodate rationed products normally used in the making of most home-canned foods.

Community groups united in an effort to save and produce foods for their families.

At the same time that women were being encouraged to do "men's jobs", manufacturers were running ads talking about when "Rosie the Riveter becomes Rosie the Housewife".

Norman Rockwell's "Rosie" became very well known and was the first visual image of "Rosie" that was widely publicized.

Women in the Workforce

Rosie at your service

"Rosie the Riveter" was a fictional woman who became one of the most well-known icons on the home front during WWII. She represented the more than six million women who worked in factories building planes, tanks, bombs and other weapons. Her name and image, in a variety of ways, were used by the United States government to encourage women to join the work force.

The name "Rosie the Riveter" was first used in a song written by Redd Evans and John Jacob Loeb. Kay Keyser was one of many who sang the song, which went on to become a national hit. Artists, like Norman Rockwell, also provided their own versions of the famous "Rosie."

Women working in the defense industry became known as "production soldiers," doing their part to win the war.

1943 TEXACO

Pretty women, with makeup on and styled hair, were most often chosen for photos and posters of female defense workers.

One line from the popular "Rosie the Riveter" song said, "… that little frail girl can do more than a man can do."

Women had to become "Jills of all trades" and do a variety of jobs previously seen as "men's work."

Bandannas were often worn in factories to cover the hair and keep it safely out of the way.

Norman Rockwell

© 1943 THE NORMAN ROCKWELL FAMILY ENTITIES

Women in the Workforce

We can do it!

With so many men enlisted in the service, women were called upon to work outside the home. The number of women who worked outside the home went from 25 percent before the war to 36 percent during the war.

These women had to work hard to prove themselves, especially to men. As they did their jobs in factories, on farms, in lumber mills, in government jobs and many other occupations, women came to be respected and seen as good workers.

Women took their roles in the workforce very seriously and paid close attention to detail to make sure their job was done to perfection.

Brothers, sons and sweethearts overseas were often on women's minds as they worked.

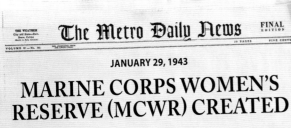

The Metro Daily News

FINAL EDITION

THE WEATHER
City and State—Rain.
Snow. Colder.
Death in Belo Almanac

VOLUME 97 — No. 786

19 PAGES   FIVE CENTS

JANUARY 29, 1943

MARINE CORPS WOMEN'S RESERVE (MCWR) CREATED

Women were called upon to learn new skills to work in environments like power plants and factories.

The government issued many posters with patriotic slogans to encourage women to join the work force.

Women in the Workforce

Child-care challenges

During the early war years, the government did not encourage mothers of children under the age of 14 to work, but as the war went on, the demand for workers rose. As women with children entered the work force, the government began to support the idea of nurseries, day-care centers and extended school services.

Some companies built their own day-care centers. For example, at one time, Kaiser Shipbuilding Company ran a 24-hour child-care center that served approximately 4,000 children.

Eleanor Roosevelt was very supportive of government- and company-run centers, designed to help working mothers find good quality care for their children.

By 1943, the need for workers had become so great, that women with children under age six were joining the work force.

Much time and preparation went into providing good nutritious food for children being cared for at day-care centers all over the nation.

With fathers serving in the military and mothers working outside the home, children became accustomed to bundling up and leaving home for the day (or even night!).

Everyday Life

In the neighborhood

The spirit of neighborhood friendship was encouraged by concern about the war and for those gone from the community into military service. The visit of the mailman each day was a welcome sight for those looking for a letter from loved ones in the service. It was common for the mail carrier to make a special effort to greet those he came in contact with. Neighbors who knew each other would check on each other to make sure their needs were met.

The neighborhood doctor was often familiar with his patients' needs so that treatment was accurate and efficient in caring for those of the community.

An afternoon ride for the children often turned a coaster wagon into a grocery cart during a visit to the neighborhood grocery store.

The local market was a good place to visit and catch up on the latest news.

What Made Us Laugh

"Watch me drive him crazy—
I'm a ventriloquist."

"I don't like the look of this! He
keeps asking are we finished?"

"Just let me know when
it gets excruciating."

"I have a serious labor problem. I don't suppose
you'd care to refuse to pay your check?"

"Well, quite a day! 7483 points.
Did we make any money?"

"Now, who do you suppose is going
to pay for that window?"

"I had another one of my spells this morning.
Everything went black and I shook all over just like a leaf."

© GETTY IMAGES

President Franklin D. Roosevelt sits alongside the Allied Supreme Commander Dwight Eisenhower as they fly to the Cairo Conference in November 1943.

© LIBRARY OF CONGRESS, PRINTS AND PHOTOGRAPHS DIVISION, FSA 8E01229

President Franklin D. Roosevelt rides in a U.S. Army jeep as he reviews American troops in Casablanca, Morocco.

Wartime President

Franklin D. Roosevelt

By the latter part of 1943, it was becoming increasingly evident that the Allies would defeat or stalemate Nazi Germany. In November, President Franklin D. Roosevelt met with Great Britain's Winston Churchill and Chinese leader Chiang Kai-shek at the Cairo Conference. He then traveled to Tehran to confer with Churchill and Russian leader Joseph Stalin.

At the conference, Roosevelt mapped out his plans to invade France and for a postwar international organization. Roosevelt's travels that year made him the first United States president to visit a foreign country during wartime. Other war discussion included a meeting with Churchill and Chiang Kai-shek in ways to defeat Japan.

Also in 1943, Roosevelt appointed Gen. Dwight Eisenhower as supreme commander of the Allied forces, dedicated the Jefferson Memorial and signed the withholding tax bill into law.

© LIBRARY OF CONGRESS, PRINTS AND PHOTOGRAPHS DIVISION, CPH 3C17121

© LIBRARY OF CONGRESS, PRINTS AND PHOTOGRAPHS DIVISION, CPH 3C05744

President Roosevelt with Maj. Gen. George S. Patton, Jr. (far right), affixing the Congressional Medal of Honor upon Brig. Gen. William H. Wilbur in the presence of Gen. George C. Marshall (far left).

© GETTY IMAGES

President Franklin D. Roosevelt confers with Gen. Douglas MacArthur, Adm. William Leahy and Adm. Chester Nimitz, who is pointing out strategic positions on a map of the Pacific War zone.

The efficiency of industry in the United States made it possible for warfare to continue unabated on demand as supplies continued to arrive as needed. Through advanced transportation, parts, materials and sub-assemblies came to large war plants from hundreds of factories across the nation.

Service at Sea

United States war officials breathed a sign of relief in the early hours of Feb. 8, 1943 when the Japanese completed a crucial evacuation of their surviving ground troops after fighting a brutal air-sea-land battle against United States troops at the island of Guadalcanal. The dogfight was the first major Allied offensive of the Pacific War.

At sea, the campaign featured two major costly battles between aircraft carriers that proved to be more costly to the Americans than to the Japanese. It involved many submarine and air-sea actions that ultimately gave the Allies an advantage.

In November, the United States initiated its second offensive, this in the very critical central Pacific region.

The Battle of Tarawa between Nov. 20 and Nov. 23 was the first time in the war that the United States faced a serious amphibious landing. The 4,500 Japanese defenders were well-supplied and well-prepared. Their tenacious fighting brought about a heavy toll on the United States Marine Corps.

Other 1943 highlights included United States victory over Japan in the Battle of Bismark Sea, and capturing and ending of Japanese occupation of the Aleutian Islands.

The sturdiness of advanced American production allowed United States-made ships and weapons to prevail over the attacks of weaker enemy weapons.

"Good heavens! What do you suppose I said!"

The importance of disciplined training from Boy Scout involvement compared military success and its medals to that first earned during merit service in scouting.

War Machines

Airplanes we flew

The Memphis Belle, nickname for a B-17 Flying Fortress was the first United States heavy bomber to complete 25 missions over enemy territory during World War II. The bomber deployed to Prestwick, Scotland, to a temporary base and then to its permanent base at Bassingbourn, England. Capt. Robert Morgan's crew flew 29 combat missions with the 324th Bomb Squadron; only four of them were with aircraft other than the Memphis Belle.

The Memphis Belle and crew gained notoriety when it inspired the making of a 1944 documentary film, *Memphis Belle: A Story of a Flying Fortress* and *Memphis Belle*, a 1990 Hollywood feature film.

The plane, which was named for Morgan's sweetheart, Margaret Polk of Memphis, Tenn., is currently undergoing extensive restoration at the National Museum of the United States Air Force in Dayton, Ohio.

The success of United States fleets was advertised to be due to the quality construction carried out by Oldsmobile, a division of General Motors. Car makers shut down automobile production and took up aircraft manufacturing in assistance with the war effort.

The look of a confident pilot was used by Champion Spark Plugs to advertise the importance of dependable equipment in military success.

The Memphis Belle crew shown at an air base in England after completing 25 missions over enemy territory on June 27, 1943, were left to right: Tech. Sgt. Harold P. Loch, top turret gunner; Staff Sgt. Cecil H. Scott, ball turret gunner; Tech. Sgt. Robert J. Hanson, radio operator; Capt. James A. Verinis, co-pilot; Capt. Robert K. Morgan, pilot; Capt. Charles B. Leighton, navigator; Staff Sgt. John P. Quinlan, tail gunner; Staff Sgt. Casimer A. Nastal, waist gunner; Capt. Vincent B. Evans, bombardier and Staff Sgt. Clarence E. Wichell, waist gunner.

Acts of Kindness

G.I.'s making a difference

Many of the American soldiers were very compassionate to civilians around them affected by the war. It was not unusual for G.I.'s to stop and help innocent people who were injured or to assist with homeless women and children. Many would take time to search for wounded after bomb strikes and assist them with medical attention.

Often, military personnel spent time talking to children and making simple friendships with them. The tender hearts of traditionally tough-skinned soldiers were revealed when they left civilians behind they had befriended during their stay in certain areas.

Soldiers help to search the wreckage of a school in South London the day it was partially destroyed during a German bombing raid in 1943. Thirty-eight children and six teachers were killed in the raid.

American actor and comedian Joe E. Brown, sitting in the driver's seat, takes time to stop and talk to children while on sight-seeing tour in China.

Above: An American military policeman directs traffic with the help of a newly deputized young Italian boy dressed in a cut-down United States uniform and a military policeman's helmet.

FAMOUS BIRTHDAYS
Lynn Redgrave, March 8
English actress
Sly Stone, March 15 singer

In the midst of war, this young woman pauses to offer a prayer of gratefulness for God's strength and assistance from dedicated soldiers.

THE SATURDAY EVENING
POST
NOVEMBER 27, 1943   10¢

BILLION-DOLLAR
PLANE BUILDER
By ALVA JOHNSTON

A Gay Short Story
By ROBERT CARSON

Norman Rockwell

THANKSGIVING

"He explained to me that he's with Army Intelligence."

The Victory Book Campaign sought to collect books suitable for servicemen and to supplement the library services already maintained by the military at camps, posts and on ships.

VICTORY BOOK CAMPAIGN

WE WANT BOOKS

AMERICAN LIBRARY ASSOCIATION · AMERICAN RED CROSS
UNITED SERVICE ORGANIZATIONS FOR NATIONAL DEFENSE INC

REPRINTED WITH PERMISSION OF OREGON STATE ARCHIVES, OREGON STATE LIBRARY RECORDS, FOLDER 42, BOX 29

The Metro Daily News

FINAL EDITION

MARCH 29, 1943

MEAT, BUTTER AND CHEESE RATIONED IN THE U.S.

Supporting Our Troops

The Victory Book Campaign became one of the most popular ways of supporting troops. The effort, which began shortly after the United States began mobilizing huge numbers of troops in 1940, was designed to supply millions of servicemen with wholesome and educational reading material.

The books were collected through state and local libraries. The campaign was sponsored by the American Library Association, Red Cross and United Service Organization. Other assistance came from such groups as the National Education Association, Boy Scouts, Girl Scouts, Campfire Girls and League of Women voters, as well as various labor and fraternal organizations.

Books were distributed through base libraries and small groups known as "traveling libraries" which could reach some of the most remote areas.

Soldiers participating in the Oregon Victory Book Campaign collect at drop-offs for distribution to various military libraries.

Victory books found their way to the four corners of the earth, giving servicemen a satisfying diversion.

Women sort and package Victory Books at the Oregon State Library for shipment to servicemen. Volunteering gave those involved a sense of being a part of the war effort.

Chow Time

Feeding Our Troops

United States military land forces who couldn't access mess halls during duty were often fed with a "C-Ration," an individually canned pre-cooked or wet ration.

The first type of C-Ration was made up of a 12-ounce canned meat unit. Originally, there were only three variations of the main course. They consisted of meat and beans, meat and potato hash, and meat and vegetable stew. Generally speaking, C-Rations were not liked by U.S. Army or Marine forces because they considered them to be heavy and cumbersome.

A new menu item, meat and spaghetti in tomato sauce, was added in 1943. The following year such items as chopped ham, egg and potato, and meat and noodles were introduced. Soldiers were also given the opportunity to select from pork and rice, frankfurters and beans, and chicken and vegetables.

Rations distributed on the battlefield addressed human hunger pains for those isolated from normal sources of food.

1943 AMERICAN MEAT INSTITUTE

Field rations provided a lifeline to energy for hard working military personnel fighting on the battlefields.

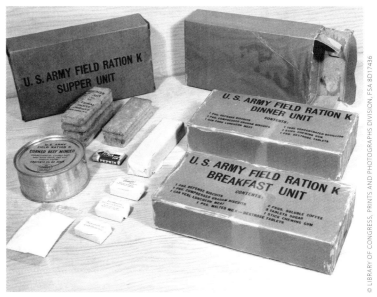

"But I blew 'Chow' four times. Maybe they just ain't hungry!"

More sophisticated food, known as K-rations, was very concentrated and was used only in time of emergency and continuous combat when regular messing facilities were not available.

Post Scripts

Dose: One Teaspoonful for Children

8:00 P.M.: Now, this medicine isn't going to hurt one bit, Elizabeth. Open your mouth, darling.

8:02 P.M.: But you want the tummy ache to be all gone tomorrow, don't you?

8:04 P.M.: You know very well it's not nasty-tasting stuff. If it were, mother would take it herself.

8:06 P.M.: But, darling, I'm not the one who's sick.

8:08 P.M.: Look here, young lady, one of us is going to take this medicine right now, and it's not going to be me!

8:10 P.M.: Come right out from under that blanket! Do you hear me?

8:12 P.M.: You're making mother very, very angry, Elizabeth!

8:14 P.M.: How do you expect me to put this spoon in your mouth if you won't hold still?

8:16 P.M.: Well, that's a fine state of affairs. All over the floor. But you're not getting out of this, young lady; there's more where that came from!

8:18 P.M.: Do you want me to call your father?

8:19 P.M.: John!

8:20 P.M.: Maybe you can do something with your child! I can't!

8:22 P.M.: Well, it serves you right for bargaining with her. She was supposed to drink it, not you.

8:24 P.M.: There now, Elizabeth. Was that so bad?

D KEY.

"May I carry your tin cans to school tomorrow?"

Lines Written 'Twixt Stove and Sink

(Apologies to Wordsworth)

SHE worked among the oft-trodden ways
  Of stove and pan and pot,
A maid whom I lament, and praise,
  And whom I miss a lot!

She took a job 'mid lathe and drill
  In wider labor marts.
Her income now makes mine look nil;
  She's making airplane parts!

Now I stay home, and scrub and sew,
  And feed the family.
I'm doing all her chores, and oh,
  The difference to me!

Yes, I make bread, while she makes dough;
  My coat's but cloth, hers, fur;
I walk, while she rides by, and oh,
  The difference to her!

Oh! "Ante-bellum status quo"
  Return. . . . I'm nothing loath!
Our lots again we'd change, and oh,
  The difference to both! —AMY GREIF.

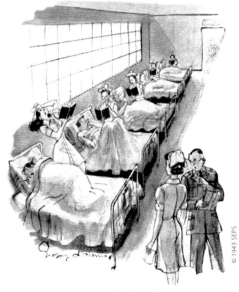

"Better transfer that former actress to something else."

"Say, what made you start talking about your girl all of a sudden? You were going great guns about the Dodgers."

To drive an Army car and keep
  His way through t'rrific traffic,
He learns by riding in a jeep
  That's autobiographic.

He's disciplined to put an end
  To habits lax or sloppy;
And, when he writes his girl, to send
  His publisher a copy.

Soon plenty tough, he yearns for fights,
  And he becomes so brave he
Insists on all the movie rights,
  And incidental gravy.

Would you today a soldier be,
  Belligerent and fiery?
Then learn to figure royalty
  And learn to keep a diary.

—JOSEPH FULLING FISHMAN

Paternal Parody

BETWEEN my dinner and bedtime,
  When the kids are losing their power,
Comes a pause for the day's recreation
  That is known as the Parents' Hour.

Forgive me for mocking the poet's sweet line,
But Longfellow's children were never like mine!

—W. W. WATT.

Take a Letter

"GOOD MORNING, Miss Diggle. Take a letter. 'Dear Mr. ——'"

"Pardon me, Mr. Grady, but I'm Miss Golden."

"Huh?"

"Miss Diggle has gone to work at the Fli-High airplane plant as a drill-press operator, and she asked me would I please fill in here until ——"

"But I just hired her last week, and she didn't say a word about contemplating a ——"

"I know. Marie—I mean, Miss Diggle, was terribly sorry she couldn't have given you more notice, but, you see, she's had her application in for some time, and then, last night, they called her and told her to report for this morning's shift—at six-thirty, mind you—and she felt she should contribute ——"

"Yes, yes. Of course. And I shouldn't be complaining. Well—uh—take a letter. 'Dear Mr. ——'"

"Oh, Mr. Grady, I'm so sorry. But I just came in this morning to tell you I can't take Miss Diggle's place. You see, I applied the other day for a position as a bus driver, and last night, right after Marie had called—well ——"

"The bus company called and asked you to report for the morning shift."

"No, I report at noon. But since I have oodles of other ——"

"I see. Well, could you spare, say, just five minutes?"

"Why, yes-s-s-s."

"Take a letter. 'Dear Mr. Waters: As soon as I can get a recap on the rear tire of my bicycle, I'll pedal over and discuss that important matter of future deliveries in full. Signed, Mr. Grady.' That will be all, Miss Diggle—I mean, Miss Fullen—no, she's the one who joined the Waacs. I mean, Miss—uh—whatever your name is."
— DALLAS R. TOBIN.

"I represent the Federal Manpower Commission. How are you fixed for help?"

"Don't care for spinach, eh?"

In a Still Small Voice

WHY don't our dear little wives
  Just cherish and coddle us?
Why do our dear little wives
  Try so hard to remodel us?

Why do they harp on our faults
  Until we grow insurrectional?
Why is the institution marriage
  Always correctional?   — THOMAS USK.

Division of Labor

HOUSEHOLDS have checks and balances,
  Husbands tell one another,
And while they attend to the balances,
  Their wives attend to the other.
— W. E. FARBSTEIN.

In Triplicate

FOR many stories there are three:
  The one that is told by me,
The one that is told by you,
And then, of course, the one that is true.
— WILMA DENNIS.

Have You Ever Noticed?

MOST players of tennis,
  Of golf and of pool,
Have a practice so common
  It's almost a rule:
After muffing a shot,
  As the best of them do,
They examine their racket,
  Their club or their cue.
But a definite fluke
  They will try to disguise
As a masterful shot,
  By concealing surprise.
It's all very childish,
  Sportsmen should shun it,
But give me a dime for
  Each time *I* have done it!
— BURGE BUZZELLE.

Granny—1943 Style
(With apologies to James Whitcomb Riley)

GRANNY'S come to our house
  And ho! my lawsy-daisy!
All the childern round the place
  Is 'ist arunnin' crazy!
Fetched a cake fer little Jake,
  And fetched a pie fer Nanny,
Fetched her ration book for ma—
  Good ol' granny!
— EVELYNE LOVE COOPER.

Excitement is always found in a young child as he takes his first steps.

Everyday Life

First-time memories

Scrapbooks with baby's first-cut lock of hair, first birthday card and first name signature represent only a few of the items that caused mothers to wipe sentimental tears and fathers to get a twinkle in their eyes. During World War II, mothers often captured special first moments in pictures or through saved items to show to dads when they returned from military service.

In 1943, such clothing items as first tie, first cuff links and first dress were big moments in early childhood memories. First school bus rides, first church recitation and earliest words all made the baby's first scrapbook that was often handed to Father when he embraced family members upon his return from war.

FAMOUS BIRTHDAYS

Max Gail, April 5 actor

Mick Abrahams, April 7 guitarist

A newborn baby receives a special salute from Dad in uniform during World War II.

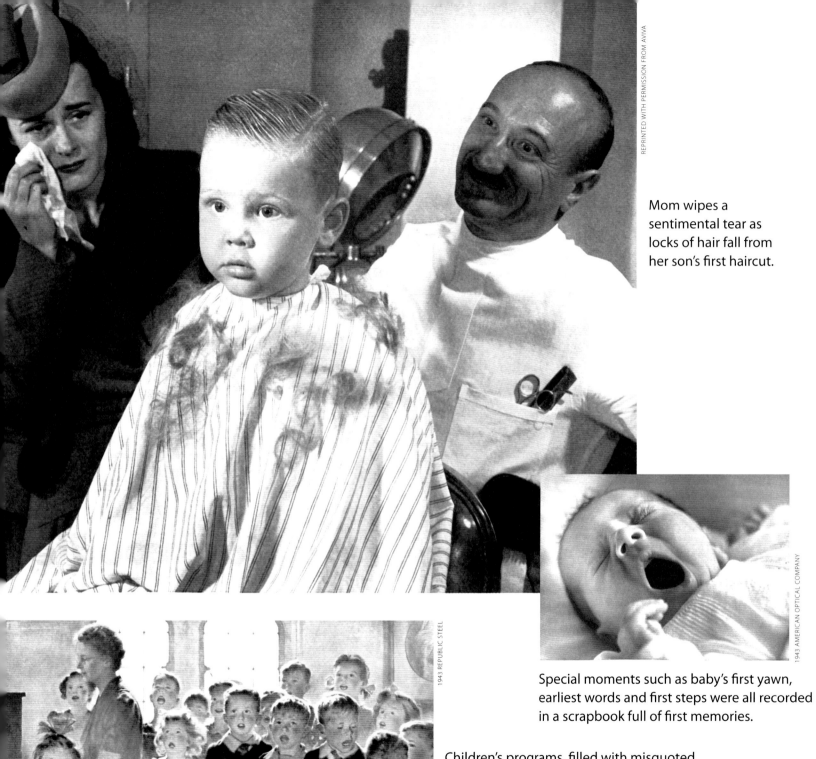

Mom wipes a sentimental tear as locks of hair fall from her son's first haircut.

Special moments such as baby's first yawn, earliest words and first steps were all recorded in a scrapbook full of first memories.

Children's programs, filled with misquoted recitations and nervous energy, were always a source of humor and memories for proud parents.

Vitamin time was always an important way of starting a healthy day of school and home activities.

Sisters sometimes made play out of what would otherwise be a painful experience, such as washing each other's hair.

Family pets were a good means of teaching how to love and care for others.

Everyday Life

Young family life

Togetherness and creativity characterized family life. With high technology and microwaves still decades in the future, family members assembled around the supper table for a special-crafted homemade meal at the end of a busy day. There, they would share the day's activities and usually enjoy a few good laughs.

In the evening, games and creative activities such as scrap booking and reading stories to each other characterized an evening bent on recognizing members of the family in their own world. Siblings often enjoyed playing outside. During the summer they would enjoy times with neighbors. In the winter, the entire family joined in with winter activities.

Of course chores were part of each family member's responsibilities. Activities such as carrying in wood, doing dishes and helping cook were all divided among children and parents.

Hand-prepared meals and snacks were personal ways that mothers shared a loving heart with family members. Anxious school children would run home to see what snack Mom had ready and waiting for them to enjoy.

"May I seize this opportunity to congratulate you on some delicious cookies!"

THE SATURDAY EVENING POST

JUNE 5, 1943   10¢

Hitler Plans for Defeat
By PETER F. DRUCKER

Task Force X
By CHARLES RAWLINGS

al moore

Arranging flowers picked from the home garden was an artistic enjoyment. Often the floral arrangement would be taken to someone in failing health or an elderly neighbor.

Favorite Pastimes

Favorite pastimes centered around enjoyment of reading, music and homemade crafts. Children enjoyed learning how to do things their parents liked to do. Reading was very popular. Children would read an entire series of books. Grandma loved to crochet or knit, often making a baby blanket or socks for servicemen. Family members often enjoyed gathering around the radio to hear episodes of *The Lone Ranger* and other radio entertainment. Neighbors would often gather for times of singing. Sometimes they would bring musical instruments and create their own neighborhood band for the evening. Of course, such evenings would usually end with homemade baked goods and a time of visiting.

The Metro Daily News

FINAL EDITION

APRIL 25, 1943

EASTER OCCURS ON THE LATEST POSSIBLE DATE

The last time was in 1886; the next time to be 2038.

Reading was a favorite activity. Trips to the local library were also a special time. Sometimes, friends would pass their favorite books around to each other.

:tening to radio programs was a popular activity, often
:companied by popcorn or homemade candy.

Knitting was very popular, whether it was making a sweater
or knitting borders around towels and handkerchiefs.

Often, families
would pull
furniture aside
and have a family
or neighborhood
dance.

Musical expression was very popular, with many
family members taking piano or voice lessons.

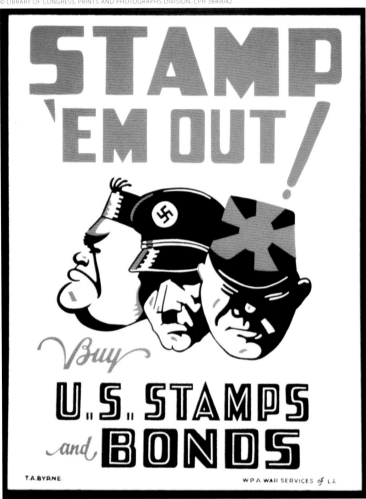

Buy War Bonds!

Series E. United States Savings Bonds were marketed by the government as war bonds between 1941 and 1980. Although there were other series, those referring to war bonds are usually referring to the Series E bonds and accrued interest for 40 years.

Bonds were generally issued at 75 cents per dollar face value and matured in a specified number of years that fluctuated with the rate of interest. Denominations available were $25, $50, $75, $100, $200, $1,000, $5,000 and $10,000.

War bonds were considered debt securities issued by a government to assist in financing military operations during times of war. They generated capital for the government and gave citizens a sense of feeling involved in their national militaries.

Posters were issued emphasizing the importance of supporting the war financially in order to give the United States an upper military position.

An elderly woman looks over a $25 war savings bond.

He Gives 100
You Can Lend 10

As seen here in the 1943 movie *Show Business at War*, actress Hedy Lamarr waits to be kissed by a soldier who has a winning roulette number while bandleader Kay Kyser (left) holds a $25 War Bond that the soldier had just won.

In a special war-bond campaign, the public school children of Chicago purchased $263,148.83 in war bonds and stamps. The funding represented enough money for the purchase of 125 jeeps, two pursuit planes and a motorcycle.

Women in Uniform

Editor's note: *The following article is an excerpt taken from "Women of Two Wars" published May 29, 1943 in* The Saturday Evening Post.

The new street uniforms of the Army nurses are very similar to those of the WAAC, which in turn were patterned after those of the Army men. But the knowing will readily spot certain differences, such as the softer and less-severe design of the nurses' caps.

The Navy Waves and the Marine Corps Women's Reserve, to carry this series of contrasts a bit further, are eligible for officers' commissions—and well-rounded wardrobes—which were beyond the reach of their respective Yeomanette and Marinette predecessors.

In developing the current crop of women's uniforms, the services sought to strike a balance between martial formality and femininity, so a girl could fit into military surroundings, yet not feel irrevocably shorn of all her maidenly graces. To achieve this, they enlisted the aid of accredited designers and stylists—like Mainbocher, who designed the uniforms of

Army Nurse (Dress Uniform)
Soon this olive drab will replace the navy blue previously worn by Army nurses.

WAFS (Women's Auxiliary Ferrying Squadron)
They have civil-service status, but get same flying suits as Army pilots.

Marine Corps Women's Reserve
Model here—Louise Stewart—happens to be bona fide MCWR lieutenant.

Navy Nurse Corps
All Navy nurses now have snappy street uniforms, stating rank of ensign.

the Waves and Spars (Coast Guard). They stressed such disarming objectives as "slenderizing appearance" and "freedom of movement."

On this latter count, the ultimate has probably been reached in a two-piece field slack suit for Army nurses—illustrated on this page—which offers enough freedom of movement for a rodeo rider or a steeplejack.

As an all-round testimonial, the epitome may be this unofficial statement by a recently enrolled Wave. "I made up my mind to join," she said, "when I saw that dress uniform. A good two-piece blue suit is one of the most valuable things a girl can own. I can detach the insignia after the war, and get at least three or four years' good wear out of it."

Army Nurse Corps Field uniform "for service in theater of operations." Note big "cargo" pockets.

AC (Women's Army iliary Corps) orm of an iary—rank esponding to ate.

AWVS (American Women's Voluntary Service) One of the most widely seen non-military women's uniform.

Red Cross Field Worker in Military and Naval Welfare Services, for soldiers here and abroad.

WAVES (Women Appointed for Volunteer Emergency Service) Unlike Yeomanettes, they may get commissions. This is lieutenant, j.g.

Factory Guard This uniform is unofficial, but appropriate enough, for all that.

Women in Uniform

Nurses in the Military

Many nurses were willing to sacrifice comforts of home in order to care for those in armed forces during World War II. Women in nursing were willing to leave boyfriends, family and blossoming careers in order to kneel by the side of wounded soldiers in the midst of enemy fire on active battlefields.

For their service during World War II, 1,600 Army nurses and 565 WACS received combat decorations, including the Distinguished Service Medals, Silver Stars, Bronze Stars, Air Medals, Legions of Merit, Commendation Medals and Purple Hearts.

1943 UPJOHN

Women in nursing uniforms gave up many of their hearts' desires in order to serve wounded soldiers during World War II.

FAMOUS BIRTHDAYS

Terry Allen, May 7
Country music singer
Joe Namath, May 31
football player
Sharon Gless, May 31 actress

Grateful family members present a box of candy to a nurse in appreciation for her care of their loved one in service.

rses wrap medical supplies in
ophane to protect them during
ficult war conditions.

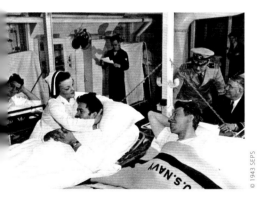

rses care faithfully for soldiers in
ercrowded military hospitals.

THE SATURDAY EVENING

POST

OCTOBER 23, 1943   10¢

**We Must Save
Free Enterprise**
By VICE-PRESIDENT WALLACE

Burma Bomber
By PETE MARTIN

Special care and warmth is given to an American soldier recovering from a battle
wound. A nurse's compassion was appreciated by injured service personnel located in
hospitals thousands of miles away from home.

"I've got to beat my brains out
like that every time I'm hungry?"

"She says if you're King, we can start calling her 'Princess'!"

"Something's wrong with my plumbing."

"I don't believe it!"

"I'm afraid you misunderstand. I'm NOT looking for a job as hired man; I'm making a help survey for the Government."

Everyday Life

Our family pet

Family pets were especially comforting during the war when they provided companionship for those lonely while loved ones were at war. They offered friendship to children who missed fathers and brothers and a sense of closeness to the elderly, especially those longing for the return of their children. Taking care of the pets gave family members a sense of responsibility and enjoyment.

A good listening pet was often utilized for special chats about lonely times or misunderstood moments. Their sense of protectiveness and loyalty easily won the hearts of other family members during family picnics and other special family outings.

Irish Setters always provided good-natured companionship. Their relaxed demeanor allowed them to fit into any type of family setting.

Dalmations were great family dogs because of their sense of interactiveness with family members. Larger families especially appreciated them for their playful, exercising fun.

Scottish Terriers were very loyal to their owners and extremely playful, especially when they were younger.

Large dogs like Great Danes and St. Bernards appeared to be imposing but were really easy going and steady-tempered in family circles. Still, their appearance often provided a sense of protection for those not familiar with them.

The barbershop was a great place to sit down and enjoy the latest comic book.

Even young boys liked to impress pretty girls with their physical prowess.

Drawing and painting were especially fun if you were lucky enough to have an easel.

Everyday Life

The fun we had

Even though metal and steel were being rationed during the war years, there were still toys available to buy. Paper dolls, for example, were at the height of their popularity during the war years, providing hours of fun for little girls. Art supplies also allowed kids to have fun and be creative.

The war also influenced playtime. Patriotic themes began to show up in comic books, and there were even new trading cards called "America at War."

REPRINTED WITH PERMISSION OF PAT LAY WILSON

© 1943 SEPS

Everyday Life

The games we played

Playing board games was a popular pastime. It was a good mixer for connection between generations as grandparents and grandchildren enjoyed playing such games as checkers, Monopoly and Clue. Card games such as Old Maid and Rook entertained families for an entire evening.

Families would gather for cookouts and homemade ice cream to play such games as croquet and badminton. Boys would gather in back lots or open fields to play softball or football.

Bobbing for apples, "Andy Over" and hide-and-seek were also favorite party outside activities.

Checkers was always a popular game for grandparents to play with grandchildren. What could be better than to spend an afternoon playing checkers.

School recess was always the best part of the day. Whether it was playing on the slide, in the sandbox or playing on the bars, it was great to have a break from studies.

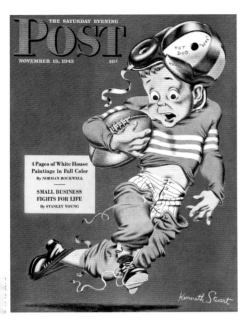

Boys loved to head to an old lot to play football or softball with teams forming neighborhood rivalries.

Deciphering a cryptic arrangement of symbols was always a good way to learn the art of logical thinking.

THE SATURDAY EVENING POST

OCTOBER 30, 1943   10¢

George VI
The King Nobody Knows
—
POWER POLITICS
SUCCEEDED IN ITALY
By DEMAREE BESS

Bobbing for apples was a fun part of outside parties, especially in the fall.

"He's leaving on a 10-day pass."

Attending dance clubs with a special girl was an option for soldiers looking to socialize off base for a few hours.

The Metro Daily News

FINAL EDITION

MAY 13, 1943

GERMAN AFRIKA KORPS AND ITALIAN TROOPS IN NORTH AFRICA SURRENDER TO ALLIED FORCES

In the Military

Enjoying time off

The excessive emotional and mental strains of military life made it more than necessary for those enduring the hardships of war to seek moments of relief and relaxation away from the rigors of the battlefield.

Often, soldiers would visit bars or dances in towns close to their bases. If they had more time off, they would sometimes tour the area close to where they were stationed. On rare occasions, they would be able to spend a few days at home before returning to their post.

Enjoying the friendship of ladies in nearby communities was always a morale booster to those in the military a long way from America.

American actress Bette Davis smiles as she serves a slice of cake to United States Army Private Vazquez while helping Allied troops in the Stage Door Canteen in New York City. Notice the excitement on Vazquez's face as he meets Ms. Davis.

Wartime Romance

The war years changed courtship and marriage, hastening both processes. Couples were more likely than ever to rush through a courtship into marriage. Marriage rates climbed above pre-war levels.

Couples could expect to spend many months or even years apart, so they made the most of their time together. Many newlyweds only had a day or two for a honeymoon before the new husband had to ship out.

1943 PALMOLIVE

Wartime artwork and photos often romanticized images of a soldier and "his girl."

REPRINTED WITH PERMISSION FROM RUSSELL STOVER CANDIES

Coming home on furlough meant making the most of the chance for a fun date.

FAMOUS BIRTHDAYS
Richard Smalley, June 6 chemist and Nobel Prize laureate
Joan Van Ark, June 16 actress

Soldiers carried pictures of their girls, enjoying a glimpse whenever they could find the time.

Due to rationing of cloth and textiles, war brides often wore basic satin gowns without frills or lace, even sharing them with other brides.

© 1943 S

JOHN
FALTER

Letters From Loved Ones

At war, there was nothing more important to military personnel than the arrival of mail. At home, family, lovers and close friends waited to hear the latest from their loved ones serving the nation in harm's way.

Emotionally powerful letters were written to counteract fear of loss and injury during battle. Letters including the reassurance of loved ones was one of the few consoling experiences during days of extreme uncertainty.

It was the flow of mail that kept military personnel the most connected to home. Civilians were encouraged to write their servicemen and women about even the most basic activities. Daily routines, family news and local gossip kept the armed forces linked to their communities.

Lynn Massman, wife of a second class petty officer who was studying in Washington, D.C, wrote letters while her baby was having an afternoon nap.

Some soldiers shared news from home with each other while others chose to be alone as they reflected about those whom they loved.

The Metro Daily News

THE WEATHER

FINAL EDITION

JUNE 30, 1943

FIVE CENTS

CIVILIAN CONSERVATION CORPS (CCC) IS ABOLISHED

Coming Home on Leave

Coming home on leave was a time of intense mixed emotions. There was the overwhelming joy of reuniting with family and loved ones and the piercing agony of separation upon return. During the brief furlough, soldiers spent most of their time visiting and enjoying great homemade meals. In many cases, there was the constant juggling act of visiting with family and attempting to salvage all of the time possible with a special love of the heart. Even during leave, soldiers in uniform were expected to uphold the respect of the United States military by example.

Uniforms were always treated with ultimate respect in display and handling.

FAMOUS BIRTHDAYS
Geraldo Rivera, July 4
reporter and talk show host
Joel Siegel, July 7 film critic
Arthur Ashe, July 10
tennis player

Nothing could describe the overwhelming joy of walking through the gates of the home place after a long period of time away from home.

Feelings of love and romance for that special person were immediately rekindled upon embrace.

After all of the heartwarming times together in a short period, separating was always a very painful experience.

A mother's loving touch was always a special part of peaceful relaxation during a welcome stay at the home scene.

"Am I having trouble today!
Every time I whistle he shows up."

Young masters sometimes had a difficult time giving up a dog that had been trained for service in World War II.

Private First Class Norman Diamond of Brooklyn gives a congratulatory pat to "Staff Sergeant Basic" and "Private First Class Adler" who have just received promotions under the authority of Dog Land.

War Dogs

Canines to the rescue

During World War II, shortly after the bombing of Pearl Harbor, the American Kennel Club and a new group calling itself Dogs for Defense rallied dog owners across the country to donate quality animals for the Quartermaster Corps. Dogs donated by the public to the U.S. Army saved the lives of many soldiers in combat.

At first, estimates indicated that 200 dogs would be needed, but that soon sharply increased. Dogs for Defense worked with qualified civilian trainers who volunteered their services without pay to train dogs for the program.

The Quartermaster Corps trained dog handlers, most of which were Quartermaster soldiers, as well as dogs. Of the 10,425 dogs trained, around 9,300 were for sentry dogs. Trained sentry dogs were issued to hundreds of military organizations. The largest group were trained in 1943 and issued to the Coast Guard for beach patrols guarding against enemy submarine activities.

U.S. Marine Raiders and their dogs, which were used for scouting and running messages, start off for the jungle front lines on Bougainville in November of 1943.

Dogs were employed and trained to indicate the presence of a hidden enemy, especially in ambush situations.

"How about something real nice in khaki, with shirts, socks, overcoat, hat and everything to match?"

One can only imagine what Norman Rockwell was trying to portray with this June 26, 1943 *Post* cover. It looks as though Pvt. Willie Gillis was having some fun taking a little rest and relaxation from his military duties.

"I hope you're not angry with me for taking you away from your friends!"

"No, thanks! The walk'll do us good."

"You can't leave for camp next week?
Well, how about the week after next?"

"Holmes is certainly doing his best to be
recommended for Officer's Training."

"One of us must whistle. It's expected of us."

Greyhound buses were credited for aiding in speeding up the job of both civilians and those in uniform in keeping wartime transportation efficient.

The bus door was also a sad place where soldiers on their way to their first camp said their farewells to loved ones who spent every last second with them until departure.

Two soldiers give their farewells to loved ones as they leave the bus terminal in Washington, D.C.

Transportation

Modern buses

While the military was engaged in activity in World War II, industry and business was working on a nationwide basis at home to see that soldiers were constantly fed, clothed, equipped and provided with all of the supplies necessary for top performance warfare.

Since the coordinating effort involved industries scattered across the country, the need for a massive transportation effort became necessary. The movement of manpower by a motor bus system was soon transporting up to a billion passengers a year.

A man with a kit of precision tools could only get to a bomber plant by way of a motor bus. Both the girl who worked at the arsenal and the selected soldier headed for an induction center rode modern buses to their destinations.

Mothers visiting their sons at camp, businessmen, farmers, nurses and teachers who had places to go in wartime America all utilized the bus service in order to reach their destinations.

Buses rolling into training camps with more inductees were often surrounded by those training for World War II military service.

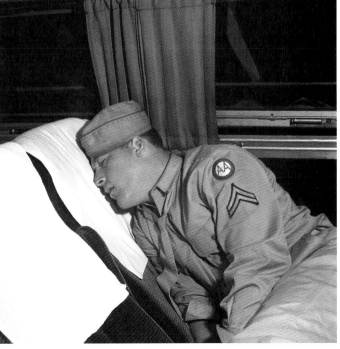

Bus transportation provided sleeping quarters for military personnel to rest during their journey to another assignment as they trained for overseas service.

The Metro Daily News

THE WEATHER
City and State—Rain.
Snow, Colder.
Clouds in their intense.

VOLUME 97 — No. 362

FINAL EDITION

20 PAGES   FIVE CENTS

JULY 10, 1943

ALLIED INVASION OF SICILY BEGINS

Codenamed Operation Husky, it was a major WWII campaign in which the Allies took Sicily from the Axis powers..

Transportation

Fast trains

Demands for speedy transportation of supplies from industry to shipyard called for a strict coordination of trains and ships. An estimated 700,000 different military items were shipped to war zones. Among those were 300 tons of ammunition, guns and army vehicles.

It was the responsibility of railroads to see to it that everything being shipped was taken to sidings exactly as needed and when needed. Any slip up or delay could hold up an entire convoy from sailing. The entire American war machine rolled into full power through the industrial progress of American manufacturers. Trains were designed to provide smooth-riding comfort and had the sturdy construction necessary for transporting army supplies and vehicles.

Santa Fe streamliner, the "Super Chief," is being serviced at the depot in Albuquerque, N.M. Servicing of these trains took five minutes.

SANTA FE 100

© 1943 SEPS

GEORGE WOLFE

"All right, then—just one more—I've got to run for it as it is."

Trains line up at a shipyard to unload American manufactured products ready to be shipped to various World War II affected countries.

1943 BUDD

All-steel trains ceased to be made during the war. However, those already manufactured continued to roll across the nation in serving the war needs of the country.

This Pennsylvania Railroad advertisement referred to railroad efficiency during war times as "The Spirit of 1943." The trains were utilized to transport large quantities of guns, planes and armaments and to handle millions of troops with precision and smoothness.

© 1943 SEPS

REPRINTED WITH PERMISSION FROM GENERAL MOTORS COMPANY

General Motors Diesel coaches transported workers to their jobs in military-equipment factories that manufactured such products as combat ships, patrol boats and landing barges.

FAMOUS BIRTHDAYS
Kathy Lennon, August 2 singer
Jimmy Johnson, August 14 football coach and television analyst

The superior performance of American military vehicles represented the superior skills of United States automobile manufacturers as they shifted the emphasis from domestic to military production.

Transportation

Military style

Automobile manufacturers halted construction of cars and converted their skill into production of military transportation and gear during WWII. Many companies utilized pre-war vehicles to transport vital materials for war factories and to rush food supplies to military bases and industrial centers.

Nearly all General Motors diesel engines were placed into military use for tanks and trucks. Others were placed into combat ships, patrol boats and landing barges. International trucks were instrumental in putting Flying Fortresses into service by rushing light and heavy loads from place to place in Boeing's short-flow, multiple-line production system.

Willy-Overland's "Go Devil" engine powered all jeeps being built for the United States Army and its allies. The superiority of the American workforce supported the country's military performance with United States manufactured vehicles.

A large fleet of International trucks helped speed the production of Flying Fortresses by rushing loads from place to place in Boeing's production system.

Willy-Overland supplied all jeeps being built for the U.S. Army with their own designed "Go-Devil" engines.

Post Scripts

Yes, and Again, No

WHEN I contemplate my soul,
I long to take a Gallup Poll.

What percentage of me truly
Can endorse this world unruly?

The wind blows cool, the sun is clear,
Eighty per cent of me gives a cheer.

Mine is the bargain dress I spied.
Ninety per cent on the pro-world side!

And I meet my love at the cocktail bar,
Dear Doctor Gallup, this world is at par.

But, oh, when luck goes into reverse,
It rains on my hat, I lose my purse;

Forget the door key and miss the train,
Concede all life is a terrible pain.

Then, with the aid of compass and chart,
I feel a statistical change of heart.

And prove that this world is no place to be,
By a very, very cross section of me.
—HORTENSE FLEXNER.

The Sea-Food Man

HIS breakfast crab,
As a general thing,
Is the cause of so much grief
That his dinner act
In the role of a clam
Is actually a relief.
—W. E. FARBSTEIN.

"I can't walk—I keep stepping on my hands."

"Now a little more to the left, and up a little."

Unfinished Sympathy

HE DIDN'T care for coffee,
It kept him wide awake;
He had, he said, no sweet tooth,
And always passed up cake.

He never owned an auto—
He couldn't learn to shift—
And thinking walking healthful,
Would not accept a lift.

He ate no steak or lamb chops,
Too costly to afford.
And what's he doing these days?
He's on the ration board.
—RICHARD ARMOUR.

Note to the Critics

WHEN I am tired of reading books
By scribbling physicians
Or ex-ambassadors or crooks,
By captains, kings or Army cooks
Or men on foreign missions;
When even Murder bores me
And Verse I can't endure,
One manuscript restores me
My faith in literature.
One opus I can turn to whose charms are
never done—
The Illustrated Catalogue of Peter
Henderson.*

*I give you Mr. Henderson and all his works
and deeds,
Who every season publishes his Catalogue of
Seeds.
Far thrillinger than Plato's,
Those passages where he dwells
On Winsall Prize Tomatoes
And Canterbury Bells.*

My heart leaps up when I behold
That style which marks the master,
In re: The Hardy Marigold
Or Giant Sunshine Aster.
His truth is fair as fiction,
His pages bright as hope,
And with what pulsing diction
He hymns the Heliotrope.
How passionate each paragraph, how purple every line
When he's discoursing on the Bean—Pole, Bush or
Stringless Vine.

*Though winds of March assail me, or February fog,
I leaf through Peter Henderson, his Garden Catalogue,
And conning Seeds Assorted
In Section 17,
Directly am transported
To summer's happy scene.*

So when upon some solemn board
The judges all are sitting
To choose, with dubious accord
For Pulitzer or some Award,
The volume most befitting,
Before the contest closes,
I nominate for fame
P. Henderson on Roses
With pictures of the same.
Yes, where's the current masterpiece, the bold
inspiring tale
To match his stirring chapter on The Culture of the Kale?

*Then here's to Peter Henderson and long may he rejoice!
The poet of the Privet Hedge, the author of my choice,
Who every dreary winter
Takes up his lyric pen
And wakes a dream of springtime
Within our hearts again.*
—PHYLLIS MCGINLEY.

*If trade names you desire to alter,
For HENDERSON read STUMP & WALTER,
JACKSON & PERKINS, BURPEE, KRAUSS,
Or any other gardening house.

"Suppose we refund your money, send you another one, without charge, close the store and have the owner shot— would that be satisfactory?"

Music Hath Charms

Waacs, surfeited with musicians, ask for some cooks.
—Headline in The Times.

WHEN lovely woman joins the colors
And marches blithely off to war,
Assignment to the cakes and crullers
Is not what she enlisted for.
No, no. These hearts, however martial,
On kitchen combat never planned.
Contrariwise, each warrior's partial
To tooting trumpet in the band.

Hey, diddle, diddle,
The big bassoon.
It's up the fiddle
And down the spoon.
It's down the skillet
And up the sax.
When girl meets oboe
She joins the Waacs.

Now ladies put aside the ladle
To bend, assiduous, the bow.
Now hands that erstwhile rocked the cradl
Twiddle the sprightly piccolo.
Farewell, the floured rolling pin
Wielded by marriageable lasses.
Now woman's place is somewhere in
Between the woodwinds and the brasses.

Hey, nonny, nonny,
The fine French horn.

Speaking of Figures

FEMININE arithmetic
Is somewhat inexact.
Yet many a girl
Who cannot add
Can certainly distract.
—ARNOLD H. GLASOW.

"I thought I'd better call you, doctor. We started playing some parlor games and—"

"Don't be so lazy, George. Bury it for him!"

Who's Telling This Joke, You or Me?

"SHALL I tell him the one about the fellow who bought the lampshade, Marge?"

"Oh, that's a swell one, Bill. . . . You'll die when you hear this, Fred. . . . Go ahead, darling."

"Well, it seems there was this guy who needed a lampshade ——"

"He was a streetcar conductor, dear."

"Oh, yes, he was a streetcar conductor; I forgot. Anyway, there was this guy—this streetcar conductor, see, Fred, who needed this lampshade—so he goes into a department store ——"

"And it was almost closing time, Bill ——"

"Yes, it was almost closing time."

"And he asks the clerk for a pink lampshade ——"

"And he asks the —— Shall I tell this, Marge, or do you want to tell it?"

"No, darling, you go ahead; you're doing fine."

"So he asks the clerk for a pink lampshade, see, Fred? And the clerk says to the customer ——"

"You forgot about the conductor not having any money, Bill. He forgot his wallet."

"Yeh, yeh, he forgot his wallet, too, Fred, so ——"

"The clerk was waiting on the conductor's mother-in-law just before this, darling, remember?"

"Yeh, that's right. So the clerk says, 'What color pink lampshade did you wish, sir?' And the guy ——"

"No, he said, 'We haven't a pink one. Do you want a baby-blue one?' thinking he was buying it for a nursery, and the conductor said ——"

"'Is that my mother-in-law you just waited on?' he said."

"No, Bill, he said, 'Who was that pill you just waited on?' and the clerk replied ——"

"'I forgot my wallet.'"

"No, that's what the conductor said, dear."

"Yeh. Well, Fred, in the end the conductor, after he's learned about his wallet and mother-in-law, he says to the clerk, 'I am going home.' Get it? 'I am going home.' Ha-ha-ha, ha-ha!"

"Fred's not laughing, dear."

"Ha-ha-ha, ha-ha! I am going home. Ha-ha-ha!"

"Amazing the way Bill can kill a joke."

—TED KEY.

© GETTY IMAGES

President Franklin D. Roosevelt officially dedicated the Jefferson Memorial on April 13, 1943. That day was also significant because it was the 200th anniversary of Jefferson's birth.

America Builds

The government broke ground for the Pentagon, the world's largest office building on September 11, 1941 (ironically). One of the main requirements was that a minimal amount of steel was to be used; instead, they used 680,000 tons of sand to build the reinforced concrete structure.

The Jefferson Memorial, which is modeled after the Pantheon in Rome, was approved by an Act of Congress in 1934. It features a 19-foot-tall statue of Jefferson and five quotations from Jefferson's writing around the interior.

© CORBIS

The Pentagon, headquarters of the United States Department of Defense, was dedicated on January 15, 1943. Located in Arlington, Virginia, it was completed in approximately 16 months and cost 83 million dollars.

Due to metal shortages during the war, the statue of Thomas Jefferson, which was supposed to be bronze, was instead cast in plaster and painted to look like bronze. The finished bronze statue was not installed until 1947.

Left to right: Joseph Stalin, Franklin D. Roosevelt and Winston Churchill. The first WWII conference of key Allied leaders—Roosevelt, Stalin and Churchill—occurred at The Tehran Conference of 1943. The leaders were meeting to discuss the opening of a second front in Western Europe, as well as war strategies against Hitler and Nazi Germany.

© CORBIS

© LIBRARY OF CONGRESS, PRINTS AND PHOTOGRAPHS DIVISION, CPH 3A3

Left to right: Gen. Chiang Kai-Shek, President Franklin D. Roosevelt and Madame Chiang Kai-Shek. Madame Chiang Kai-shek, wife of Gen. Chiang Kai-shek of China, came along to translate for her husband during the Cairo summit meetings (November 22–26, 1943). Madame Kai-shek graduated from Wellesley College in 1917, and was fluent in English. With her translation assistance, Gen. Chiang discussed the war with Japan and future hopes and plans for Asia with Roosevelt and Churchill.

World Events

Leaders in the news

By the summer of 1943, the Allies had driven the Germans out of North Africa and Allied forces had landed in Sicily. This led to the ouster of Italy's leader, Benito Mussolini.

Roosevelt and Churchill met in Cairo from November 22–26, 1943 with General Chiang Kai-shek, who became Chairman of the Nationalist Government of China on August 1, 1943. In 1942, Chiang had been named the Supreme Commander of the Allied forces in the war zone in China.

From November 28 through December 1, the "Big Three" Allied leaders met at the Tehran conference to discuss, among other things, strategies for what was to be one of the pivotal events of the war in Europe—D-Day.

On July, 25, 1943, Benito Mussolini (known as Il Duce), was dismissed as the leader of Italy by The Fascist Grand Council, which included his foreign minister and his son-in-law. They stripped him of power and had him arrested, thus ending the Fascist dictator's rule of more than two decades.

The Home Front

Men at work

Specialized skills of the American workforce were utilized keenly to assist construction for the United States cause during World War II. The training of the country's workforce was individualized for specific work on war machinery, vehicles and supplies. American technology developed the pneumatic tire that enabled the soldier to move with a swiftness never realized before in warfare.

Professional mechanics inspected and approved military vehicles and tanks before they were shipped to the battlefields for use. Many of the military vehicles were cared for by professionals trained with a Doctor of Motors, enabling them to skillfully work on hydraulic breaks and to repair trucks, tractors and jeeps. For that reason, they were often referred to as "Master of a thousand crafts."

Need for military construction bolstered the workforce and provided an abundance of jobs toward the war effort for those at home.

REPRINTED WITH PERMISSION OF MAHLE CLEVITE

American engineers and designers were responsible for developing the best means for utilizing the country's skillful workforce in war manufacturing.

WE WOULD LIKE TO ACKNOWLEDGE AND THANK PHILLIPS-VAN HEUSEN CORPORATION, THE OWNER OF THE VAN HEUSEN AND ARROW TRADEMARKS

WE WOULD LIKE TO ACKNOWLEDGE AND THANK PHILLIPS-VAN HEUSEN CORPORATION, THE OWNER OF THE VAN HEUSEN AND ARROW TRADEMARKS

Executives gathered to discuss ways to convert certain kinds of domestic manufacturing into war production.

TO POP
FATHERS DAY

PLANT 46

VARD SCOTT

© 1943 SEPS

laborers occasionally pulled a surprise from their dinner bucket that they carried with them to the factory each morning.

Specialized skills that had been used in the manufacturing of home products were converted to war production.

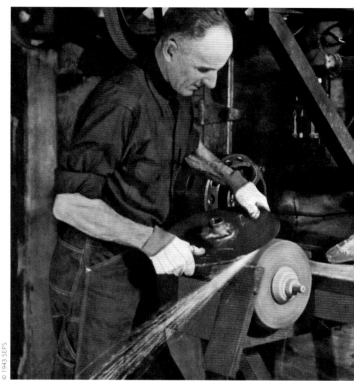

© 1943 SEPS

THE GOODYEAR TIRE & RUBBER COMPANY

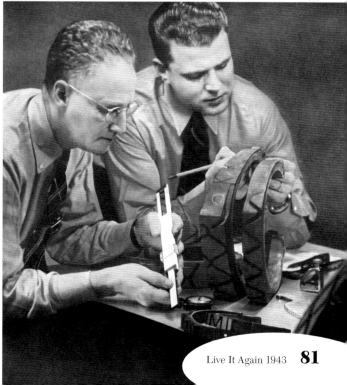

The use of rubber in manufacturing was an important part in the superior performance of jeeps, tanks and even the footwear of American soldiers.

Military personnel worked night patrol in case enemies attempted to approach encampments during the night.

United States forces planned nighttime military strikes to catch enemy troops off guard.

Working at Night

Home and abroad

Nighttime work was common in 1943 both on the war and domestic scenes. Many military advancements were made during dark hours in an attempt to catch enemy forces off guard. Soldiers stood guard duty at night and learned to recognize the sounds of potential enemies approaching in the dark.

On the home front, the improvement of tractor lights allowed farmers to work in fields well past sunset. Working late was especially prevalent on farms where one or more loved ones who normally shared in the workload were gone on war assignments. Factories manufacturing military supplies ran assembly lines around the clock in order to keep equipment needs flowing at a quick speed.

Improved streetlights allowed children to stay out after dark and play games with friends in the neighborhood.

1943 BORG WARNER INDUSTRY

1943 REPUBLIC STEEL

New and improved lights on farm machinery allowed field work to continue long after sunset.

The Metro Daily News

FINAL EDITION

THE WEATHER
City off State—Nice.
State, Color.
Down a Nice state.

20 PAGES   FIVE CENTS

VOLUME 42 – No. 243

AUGUST 5, 1943

JOHN F. KENNEDY AND CREW ARE FOUND

Soloman Islanders coastwatchers, Biuku Gasa and Eroni Kumana rescue crew with their dugout canoe.

Everyday Life

Enjoying family and friends

With so many shortages and so much rationing, families had to make their own fun at home and in their own neighborhoods. Visiting with family and friends, as well as listening to the radio together, were popular pastimes.

Playing cards became much more popular, along with board games. People also enjoyed going to a Saturday matinee, which included newsreels and war films.

Children and families could still enjoy summer fun, like having a day at the beach or the lake. Those who lived in cities or larger towns could take a trolley or bus to the shore. In rural areas, people had to walk, ride their bikes or save ration stamps and share rides to have fun in the sun.

There was no shortage of college football games since college players usually didn't enlist until after graduation.

Neighbors enjoyed meeting up for some friendly gossip across the fence.

Sweater-clad coeds had to make time for studying (or not!), despite the distractions of the war years.

FAMOUS BIRTHDAYS
Ted Neeley, September 20
  actor and singer
Ian Ogilvy, September 30
  English actor

A day at the beach, playing cards with the gals, lost its appeal with so many of the guys off to war.

A hunting trip always provided time for family interaction. Fathers often used the occasion to teach children about hunting and safety rules as well as good instruction in life principles.

Everyday Life

Outdoor fun

In a less technical world, the lure of outdoor fun in 1943 was an opportunity for creative fun in all seasons. Families loved to pack a homemade picnic lunch and head for a park or county fair. Sand-lot baseball games, hunting and camping in a make-shift tent were all part of outside activities of the time. Sand boxes were popular, as well as such games as crochet and horseshoe. Friends would frequently gather for Sunday afternoon cookouts, often with a fresh batch of homemade ice cream and fresh-picked strawberries.

In the winter, neighborhood battles erupted around homemade snow forts. Sledding down hills in the field, often ending on a farm pond, worked up an appetite for hot chocolate and homemade cookies.

A patch of grass under a shady tree on a hot summer afternoon proved to be a good spot to spend time with that special friend until the family dog discovered the favorite spot.

Canoeing and fishing on a farm pond often made the afternoon pass quickly for a group of boys looking for cheap entertainment.

School recess meant a break from studies and sometimes a friendly snowball fight between students.

CHARLES BERGER

Father and Son

Special moments

A time of playing pitch and catch in the backyard was representative of how fathers and sons learned to interact by spending time together in 1943. Sons would often work with fathers on family projects or some type of trade interaction. On the farm, sons would help fathers in the fields or in the barn.

However, the interaction between fathers and sons often went well beyond chores around the house. Activities such as hunting, fishing or playing in a local softball league often provided bonding that lasted for a lifetime. Often, activities were initiated by a father who realized his son's special interests. The role model provided by a good father was an example of good citizenship that sowed seeds for future generations.

1943 CORN REFINING COMPANY

The moment that a son learned that he had grown was a very proud moment, especially when he was measured by a man of full stature, his father.

Hunting trips were often an opportunity to learn lessons for life beyond the activity itself.

1943 WINCHESTER

"You see daddy doesn't mind taking cod-liver oil."

[Wh]en a father arrived home with a model [p]lane for his son, the boy felt like the [luc]kiest person in the world. When that [pla]ne was a replica of a model the father [ha]d flown during the war, it became [pri]celess in the son's eyes.

[F]lying model airplanes was a very popular activity in 1943. Often, several fathers and sons would gather in an open area to demonstrate their plane-flying skills.

This spoof April Fool's cover from the April 3, 1943 *The Saturday Evening Post* became a good thinking exercise for those looking for anything out of the ordinary in the photo. The clock spelling out "April Fool," the hands reaching out of the picture over the mantle, the deer sitting under the man's chair and the man wearing a roller skate were just a few of the quirks in the fun illustration.

Staying Young

Many homes in 1943 had three generations of occupants. Grandma and grandpa had their own room and assisted with chores, chipped in with everyday tasks and helped watch over and entertain the children. The idea of day-to-day contact with grandchildren was beneficial to young and old alike. The wisdom of grandparents passed on to children gave the young people helpful insights at the beginning of life. However, the youthful vitality of grandchildren paced grandparents and enabled them to still enjoy the energy and joy of the younger generation.

Grandmas who enjoyed living by the old adage, "busy hands are happy hands," could often be found knitting in a relaxing chair.

Grandpa took a special moment after school to listen to the day's activities and concerns from his grandchildren.

"Of course, to follow my plan completely they'd have to bring everybody back to the United States and start all over."

An occasional back stretch behind the scenes was appropriate for the elderly trying to keep up with youthful energy.

HOWARD SCOTT

Local men were hired to help do agricultural work that would pick up the slack for farmers and other farm-related workers who were away serving in WWII.

U.S. Crop Corps

Townspeople and farmers working together

By 1943, local and national leaders were busy organizing means to assist farms where workers were away in the war. As a result, the U.S. Crop Corps was formed to include all non-farming men who could give time to work on farms where help was needed. In addition, boys and girls between the ages of 14 and 18 could work under the umbrella of the Victory Farm Volunteers. Women worked through the Women's Land Army.

Local agricultural extension services registered the names of townspeople who would help and of farmers who needed help. Most families could keep up with the everyday maintenance of their farms but assistance was often needed for the large task of harvesting. Additional farm-labor programs gave city and town dwellers the chance to bring in the crop for the war cause and get a taste of farm life in the process.

The Women's Land Army employed women, mainly on a daily basis, to pick fruit, hoe, weed and harvest vegetables. In some cases, they assisted with processing food and helping with house work.

The mutual cooperation of paid townspeople with farmers allowed for a successful harvest of wheat and other crops.

© 1943 SEPS

THE SATURDAY EVENING

POST

AUGUST 14, 1943   10¢

The Exciting Story of America's Great Global Air Line
By MATTHEW JOSEPHSON

Where's All the Meat?
By ROBERT M. YODER

Country Gentleman

MAY, 1943 . . . FIVE CENTS

...ganizations such as
...e Women's Land Army
...nployed women on a
...ily basis to help with
...rden and fruit harvests
... well as processing food
... farm homes.

This May 1943 *Country Gentleman* cover mentions a major distribution of posters in small towns and elsewhere to assist the Department of Agriculture in enlisting townspeople in the U.S. Crop Corps.

BREAD IS JUST AS IMPORTANT AS **BULLETS**

U.S. CROP CORPS

FARM HELP IS COMING

Country Gentleman is distributing thousands of posters in small towns everywhere to help the Department of Agriculture enlist townspeople in the U.S. Crop Corps.

AMERICA'S FOREMOST RURAL MAGAZINE

The Department of Agriculture requested that a workforce of experienced farmers and agricultural workers remained in the United States in order to assist in the national flow of the food chain.

The September 25, 1943 front cover of *The Saturday Evening Post* featured the success of the nation's harvest in spite of the fact that a large sector of the workforce was away serving in WWII.

Young children contributed their share of assistance with family chores. Daughters would work alongside of their mothers with cooking and food preservation.

The Metro Daily News FINAL EDITION

SEPTEMBER 8, 1943

ITALY SURRENDERS TO ALLIED FORCES

Feeding a Nation

From the farm to the table

By 1943, it became evident that there was a growing problem of keeping the full flow of food going from the farms to the kitchen table. The drafting of many farmers and assistants had taken its toll on the normal available manpower needed to harvest and produce food for the nation's people and livestock. The Department of Agriculture attempted to keep a force of experienced farmers and agricultural workers in the land. The department also encouraged the return of workers who were not employed in essential defense industries and who had agricultural experience, especially on the large Great Plains farms.

On April 29, 1943, Congress passed Public Law 45 which established the Emergency Farm Labor Program. The new legislation gave the Extension Service in each state the responsibility of recruiting, transporting and placing agricultural workers.

In the homes, a greater emphasis was placed on canning and freezing food in order to stretch grocery budgets and save food for potential emergency times.

Congress passed a law which established the Emergency Farm Labor Program. This was especially helpful for assistance on the large Great Plains farms.

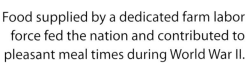

Food supplied by a dedicated farm labor force fed the nation and contributed to pleasant meal times during World War II.

© GETTY IMAGES

City Life

New York City

New York, New York—a city of approximately 7 million people in 1943, chock full of things to do. One could take in a smash Broadway play, like 1943's *Oklahoma*. There was also window shopping at Macy's and Gimbel's or a trip to the top of the Empire State building. You could do it all, despite the war.

Soldiers could stop in at the famous Stage Door Canteen for dancing, entertainment, food and non-alcoholic drinks. Celebrities like Marlene Dietrich and Helen Hunt served up sandwiches and rubbed elbows with the troops.

During WWII, more than three million troops moved in and out of the city. It came to be known as "Last Stop U.S.A." by the many men who were ready to embark across the Atlantic to fight.

In March, 1943, reportedly the peak day for the New York City port, there were 543 merchant ships anchored in the harbor. Sixty-three million tons of supplies were shipped through the port between Pearl Harbor and V-J Day.

Manhattan's skyline at night was spectacular, thanks to skyscrapers like the art-deco Chrysler Building, which stands 77 stories high. New York nightlife attracted everyone from soldiers to defense-plant workers.

© GETTY IMAGES

Rides like "The Cyclone" at Coney Island, at that time the largest amusement area in the United States, were enjoyed by all.

Penn Station was at its peak usage during WWII as troops traveled to and from their posts. Many a last kiss happened there!

Even with a war on, kids (and maybe a soldier or sailor, too!) enjoyed sled rides in Central Park.

© GETTY IMAGES

Tribute to Norman Rockwell

Norman Rockwell became a beloved, well-known artist, thanks in large part to the 323 covers he created for *The Saturday Evening Post*. His cover art portrayed the "comman man"—and his wife, his children, his pastor, his doctor, his barber, his dog and his neighbors!

Rockwell liked his characters, and he painted them with sympathy and a decent humor. Discussing his work, he said, "I guess I am a storyteller, and although this may not be the highest form of art, it is what I love to do."

Born in New York City in 1894, Rockwell spent his childhood on Manhattan's Upper West Side. *Boys' Life* hired him as an art director while he was still in his teens, and at age twenty-one, he began working as a freelance artist. His first cover appeared on the *Post* on May 20, 1916.

MISSOURI DARK MULE—By Jack Alexander

BEGINNING
THE STORY OF HELEN HAYES

When WWI broke out, Rockwell decided to enlist in the Navy. When his identity as a *Post* contributor was discovered, he was sent to New York and installed in the officers' quarters. There, he was often summoned to dinner to sketch the visitors. During this time, he was also allowed to paint *Post* covers.

After leaving the Navy, Rockwell, whose previous covers were primarily of boys, began to include people of all ages in his paintings. In his paintings, he used real people for models, people marked by life and faithfully rendered to the last wrinkle, callus, stoop and irregular nose line.

His attention to detail was unprecedented. If a setting called for a colonial bedstead or footstool, he would haunt auctions or antique shops until he found what he wanted. He kept 200-odd costumes on hand for his models, and he was constantly adding to that wardrobe.

Rockwell breathed affection into his paintings and they aroused affections in the hearts of their beholders, none more so than his series of "The Four Freedoms."

THE TERRIBLE-TEMPERED DR. BARNES

HAPPY LAND
WOES OF AN ARMY COOK

FREEDOM OF WANT

The Four Freedoms

Franklin D. Roosevelt gave a speech in 1941 that inspired Rockwell to create a series of paintings depicting "The Four Freedoms" that Roosevelt had described. He put his heart and soul into these works, and the series took him seven months to complete.

In 1943 the four paintings were published in February and March issues of the *Post*. Each was accompanied by essays by contemporary writers. The paintings were very popular and a great success. The U.S. Treasury Department and the *Post* sponsored a traveling art exhibit that toured sixteen cities. The exhibit raised $130 million dollars for the war effort through the sale of war bonds.

Rockwell's freedom series had a universal appeal for Americans during the war because, as *Post* readers often said: "He understands us."

FREEDOM OF SPEECH

FREEDOM OF WORSHIP

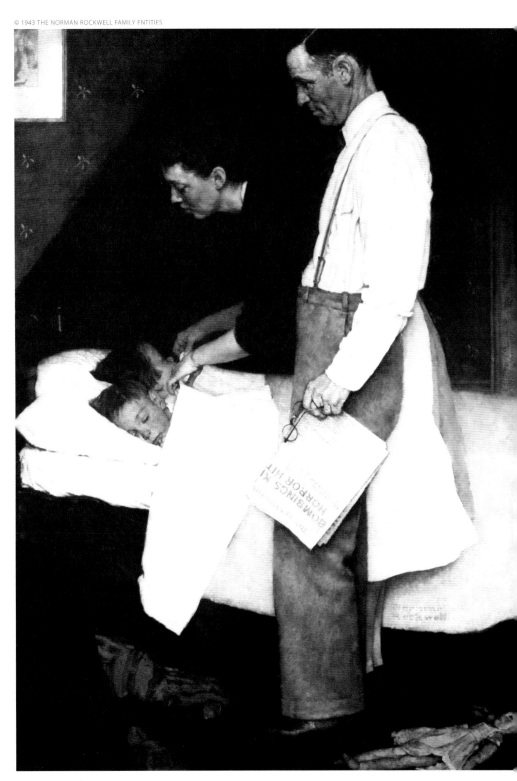

FREEDOM OF FEAR

Fashion of the Day

What children wore

In 1943, older children's clothing very often resembled styles worn by their mothers and fathers, but little children had some styles of their own. Little girls wore pinafore and dirndl-style dresses, often with rickrack or lace trim. Little boys sometimes wore shorts (but not knickers).

Junior military styles were also sold for both boys and girls, with styles like Officer's or Admiral's Suit or Uniform for Boys and "Jr. WAAC" and "Jr. WAVE" outfits for girls.

Wool was in short supply, so cold-weather clothes were often made with fabrics like rayon or "reprocessed" wool.

Beautiful, 10-year-old actress Elizabeth Taylor looks lovely in this feminine dress, a typical style from 1943. In 1943, Taylor and a young Roddy McDowell starred in the film *Lassie Come Home*.

© GETTY IMAGES

FAMOUS BIRTHDAYS
Chevy Chase, October 8
comedian and actor
Dafydd Iwan, October 24
singer-songwriter

"All I want to do is attract them enough so they'll let me play first base."

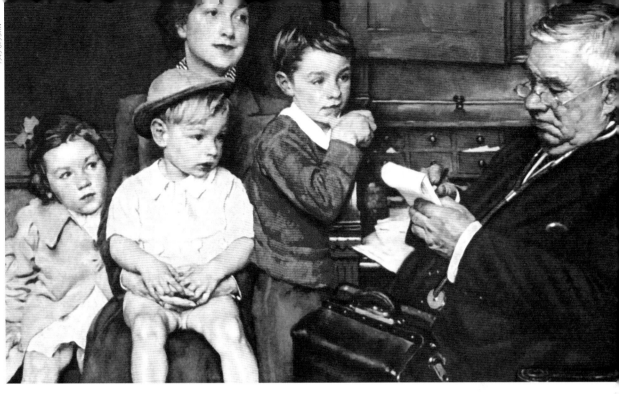

The little ones shown here are dressed in the simple styles and solid colors usually worn by children. The youngest boy is wearing shorts, a popular choice for little boys

Hats, popular with adults, were also popular for children. Little girls often wore bonnets. In cold weather, girls of all ages liked to wear head kerchiefs and boys sported knit caps.

Women would line up for hours just for the opportunity to buy a pair of leather shoes.

1943 EVERSHARP

The typical coed girl liked to wear simple sweaters and skirts to school.

Square shoulders, inspired by Hollywood, were considered smart.

Fashion of the Day

Women looking their best from head to toe

Rationing during WWII led to new styles and fabrics, but women still liked to dress well. Styles used less fabric and gabardine and rayon came into wider use.

Hats and head coverings of all kinds were popular with women, everything from pillboxes and berets to head scarves and turbans.

Traditional leather shoes required ration stamps, so retailers made "non-rationed" women's styles, which were made of gabardine and had synthetic soles.

High school and college girls had some styles of their own, including bobby sox.

A veiled hat could always make a fashion statement.

"Well, do I look dangerous?"

Fashion of the Day

Men stepping out in style

Suits and ties were the order of the day for businessmen or for any man going out for the evening; however, a man who bought a new suit in 1943 would find some changes in design. Because of fabric shortages, men's suits were designed as simply as possible with no vests (sometimes men wore knitted waistcoats or vests under their coats instead), no extra pocket flaps and, usually, no cuffs.

Men, like women, needed to use rationing coupons to buy clothing and shoes. Shoe rationing began in February 1943, allowing civilians only three pairs of leather shoes per year.

Stylish overcoats, like the Chesterfield, and a fedora or homburg hat, completed a businessman's look.

The Metro Daily News

FINAL EDITION

OCTOBER 23, 1943

BURMA RAILWAY OPENS

How to help Pop feel 20 years younger!

1 FROM EDDIE — on Father's Day! And how Pop loves 'em! Somehow, Pop is *always* short of Arrow Shorts, his favorites! Tops in comfort, they have *no center seam* to make a man squirm. (This idea is so good it's patented.) Get them in TRADEWINDS pattern. 75¢.

2 FROM MOTHER! TRADEWINDS shirts, Arrow's big June feature combination! Made of coolest light-weight fabric — in 3 widths of smart tape stripes. White and 9 colors. TRADEWINDS have latest Arrow Collars . . . "Mitoga" figure-fit . . . finest tailoring. $2.24.

3 FROM NANCY! Made to harmonize with TRADEWINDS shirts, these Arrow Ties rate No. 1 with her dates — THREE different kinds: printed foulards . . . striped Henleys . . . printed mesh — *something* NEW! ALL *stunners*, wrinkle-resistant, perfect-knotting! $1.00.

4 FROM COOKIE! (Who wouldn't be left out for worlds!) Arrow TRADEWINDS Handkerchiefs, in patterns to harmonize with Shirts and Ties. An *elegant* finishing touch! 35¢ and 50¢. See the TRADEWINDS ensemble at your Arrow dealer's! *Cluett, Peabody & Co., Inc., Troy, N.Y.*

ARROW TRADEWINDS...the smart new ensemble for Father's Day, June 20

Shirts and shorts have the "Sanforized" Label—less than 1% shrinkage

BUY U.S. WAR BONDS and STAMPS

McGREGOR

Men wore ties and dress shirts under cardigan sweaters for a more formal weekend look.

Dress shirts had pointed collars, and ties were fairly wide.

WE WOULD LIKE TO ACKNOWLEDGE AND THANK PHILLIPS-VAN HEUSEN CORPORATION, THE OWNER OF THE VAN HEUSEN AND ARROW TRADEMARKS

It wasn't just models who sacrificed comfort for style—fashion was a lot of work (and maybe a little pain at the end of the day) for women everywhere.

In the evening, women might choose to continue the glamour by relaxing at home in a peignoir set or tailored trousers and a tied-up shirt.

NAME
ELAINE BLOSSOM

SIZE   12 - 14
BUST   35½
WAIST   25
HIPS   35
HEIGHT
HAIR

© 1943 SEPS

FAMOUS BIRTHDAYS
Sam Shepard, November 5
playwright and actor
Billie Jean King, November 22
tennis player

© 1943 SEPS

Dolled-Up Dames

Sporting a little attitude

In 1943, there were lots of ways to look glamorous, but it took some time and effort. Hairstyles, for example, often meant setting the hair in pin curls overnight, and then getting up the next morning to style it.

The natural look in makeup was definitely not the norm. Women who wore makeup (not everyone did) usually wore foundation, powder and bright lipstick, along with eyebrow pencil to emphasize the brow line.

"Of course I had to tell her she looked like a million—and I meant every day of it!"

The victory roll was a popular hair style that took some time to create.

R. WEST'S MIRACLE TOOTHBRUSH

This March 20, 1943 *Post* cover image portrays how a lady wouldn't go "to town" without gloves and, perhaps, a glamorous, veiled hat.

Sporting Champions

In a rematch against the St. Louis Cardinals, the New York Yankees won their 10th World Series Championship in 21 seasons. Due to World War II, both teams' rosters were depleted. The Yankees played without Joe Dimaggio, Phil Rizzuto, Red Ruffing and Buddy Hassett. Johnny Beazley, Jimmy Brown, Creepy Crespi, Terry Moore and Enos Slaughter were missing from the Cardinals lineup.

The Chicago Bears, also known as the "Monsters of the Midway," defeated the Washington Redskins in the NFL championship game behind the quarterback skills of Sid Luckman.

In college football, Notre Dame Fighting Irish quarterback Angelo Bertelli was the Heisman Trophy winner while Count Fleet raced to a Triple Crown award in horseracing.

Winning their 10th World Series, the New York Yankees defeat the St. Louis Cardinals. The headline the next day told the story, "Chandler Wins on Dickey's Homer, 2-0." The world series program used at Yankee Stadium saluted a team where many players were serving in the military.

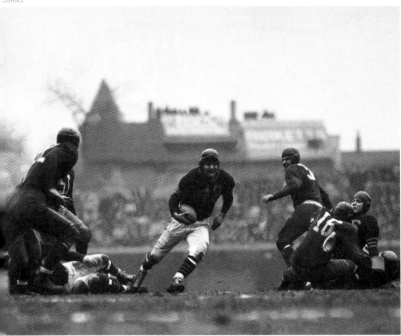

Behind the solid play of quarterback Sid Luckman, the Chicago Bears defeated the Washington Redskins, 41-21, in the NFL championship game which was played at Wrigley Field in Chicago.

Notre Dame Fighting Irish quarterback Angelo Bertelli's leadership at Notre Dame Stadium in South Bend, Ind. garnered him the famed Heisman Trophy award for 1943.

Count Fleet, winner of horseracing's Triple Crown, appeared covered with a floral wreath at Pimlico Track, near Baltimore. In 1943, he was also recognized as the "United States Horse of the Year."

"You must remember this …" *Casablanca*, starring Humphrey Bogart and Ingrid Bergman, went on to win three Oscars, including Best Picture and Best Director, and went on to capture hearts for years after its release.

Tops at the Box Office

This Is the Army

For Whom the Bell Tolls

The Song of Bernadette

Coney Island

Stage Door Canteen

Casablanca

Sweet Rosie O'Grady

Heaven Can Wait

The More the Merrier

So Proudly We Hail!

For Whom The Bell Tolls, starring Gary Cooper and Ingrid Bergman, was a top box office hit of 1943. The movie, based on a novel by Ernest Hemingway, went on to win an Oscar.

At the Movies

Movies were a great diversion and remained popular in 1943. People worked hard, and the movies were a good source of inexpensive entertainment. Many people also enjoyed the newsreels, which let them see what was happening at the war front.

After the newsreels, people wanted to be entertained, but they couldn't always forget the war. Many popular movies had war themes. For example, *Casablanca* and *For Whom the Bell Tolls* both had themes featuring the horrors of Fascism. They also had one other thing in common … Ingrid Bergman!

Ingrid Bergman was one of the most popular actresses in 1943, along with Irene Dunne, Lauren Bacall and Judy Garland. Popular actors included Humphrey Bogart, Gary Cooper, John Wayne and Errol Flynn.

Some popular actors, notably Jimmy Stewart, were not making movies in 1943; instead, they were serving in the Armed Forces.

Remember when Ronald Reagan was an actor? Here he appears with actress Joan Leslie in *This is the Army*, a wartime musical.

The Song of Bernadette was a critical and commercial success, winning four Oscars and securing nominations in eight other categories. It also made Jennifer Jones a star.

Top Hits of 1943

"I've Heard That Song Before"
Harry James

"Paper Doll"
Mills Brothers

"Sunday, Monday, or Always"
Bing Crosby

"There Are Such Things"
Tommy Dorsey

"You'll Never Know"
Dick Haymes

"Taking a Chance on Love"
Benny Goodman

"Comin' in on a Wing and a Prayer"
The Song Spinners

"In the Blue of Evening"
Tommy Dorsey

"White Christmas"
Bing Crosby

"I Had the Craziest Dream"
Harry James

"That Old Black Magic"
Glenn Miller

The Music We Loved

With gas shortages and rationing, radio became a vital form of entertainment for families in 1943. Crooners who sang in front of the bands went on to become more popular than the big bands themselves. Singers like Dinah Shore, Bing Crosby and Frank Sinatra became stars.

With so many sweethearts, sons, brothers and fathers overseas, sentimental songs became popular in 1943. For example, the popular hit "You'll Never Know," sung by Dick Haymes, was based on a poem written by a young war bride from Oklahoma, and her feelings struck a chord with Americans. Love, longing and the war were important themes that hit home.

© GETTY IMAGES

Country singer, Al Dexter, had a big hit on his hands in 1943 with "Pistol Packin' Mama."

Three of the most popular singers in 1943, (L to R) Dinah Shore, Frank Sinatra and Bing Crosby, rehearse for a radio appearance.

Betty Grable, the famous pin-up girl, married trumpeter, Harry James, in Las Vegas on July 6, 1943.

The popular Mills brothers appeared in the 1943 movie, *Reveille with Beverly*. Their hit record, "Paper Doll," was number one from November 6 through December 25, 1943.

Christmas
1943

In Washington, D.C. a sailor receives help in wrapping his Christmas gifts from assistants at the United Nations service center.

FAMOUS BIRTHDAYS
John Kerry, December 11
politician
Ben Kingsley, December 31
British actor

Those recovering from wounds were given a Christmas party in the ward of 16th General Hospital on Dec. 26, 1943.

Celebrating Christmas

In the military

The smell of ham, mashed potatoes and a full-cooked meal were usually a faraway dream for most of those serving in the military. However, on Christmas Day, it often became a reality. Where possible, soldiers were invited to large gathering places and fed a full-course meal, complete with a special dessert. The more fortunate troops would receive cards and letters, perhaps even in a Christmas box from family and friends at home.

Celebrities and volunteers would often visit troops for concerts and shows. Afterward, they would intermingle and pass out presents. Sometimes they would assist soldiers in wrapping gifts to mail back home.

For many of the wounded, Christmas was served in military hospitals. Others had sad and long days as prisoners of war in captivity behind enemy lines. Nearly everyone experienced the tug of emotions caused by the effects of separation on a major family holiday.

Christmas candy was often given to military personnel as tokens of well wishes.

A large group of soldiers gathered at a YMCA for Christmas dinner in 1943. Military personnel were often given full-course meals and some small gifts in areas where fighting ceased for Christmas day.

Family members pecked on an old typewriter or wrote letters of well wishes to their loved ones serving in WWII.

Celebrating Christmas

On the home front

The number of empty chairs representing family members away at war made Christmas in 1943 a holiday filled with mixed emotions. Those who had received good news from loved ones considered it to be a joyful Christmas. In other situations where no news had come, the day was long and sad. Neighbors and friends would often reach out to others whose family members were gone.

Families gathered together for a simple exchange of gifts and the traditional Christmas dinner. In the winter regions, there would often be the traditional ride across snow-covered fields in an old-fashioned sleigh. For the more religious, Christmas dinner was preceded by a time of prayer for safety and the nation's well-being.

Those gathering for Christmas dinner and opening of gifts around the Christmas tree often dressed in their Sunday best for the special occasion.

In places where winter had set in, a ride in an old-fashioned sleigh often signaled the arrival of loved ones for Christmas dinner.

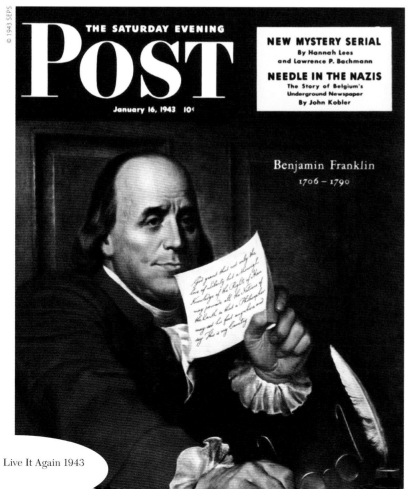

More *The Saturday Evening Post* Covers

The Saturday Evening Post covers were works of art, many illustrated by famous artists of the time, including Norman Rockwell. Most of the 1943 covers have been incorporated within the previous pages of this book; the few that were not are presented on the following pages for your enjoyment.

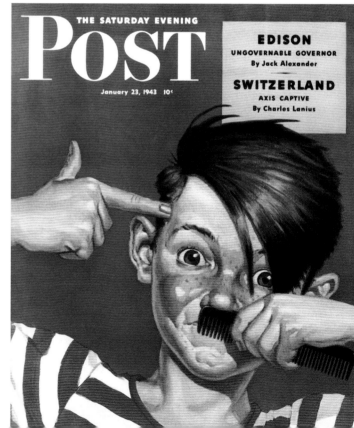

© 1943 SEPS

© 1943 SEPS

BEHIND THE SPANISH WALL – By Pete Martin

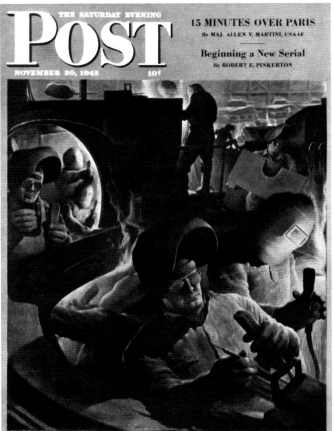

© 1943 SEPS

© 1943 SEPS

MORE FAMOUS BIRTHDAYS

January 1
Don Novello, actor

January 3
Van Dyke Parks, musician and composer

January 4
Doris Kearns Goodwin, writer

January 7
Richard Armstrong, orchestral conductor

January 10
Jim Croce, singer

January 11
Jim Hightower, radio hosT and author

January 13
Richard Moll, actor

January 15
Margaret Beckett, British politician

January 17
Chris Montez, singer

January 24
Sharon Tate, actress

January 25
Tobe Hooper, film director

January 26
César Gutiérrez, Venezuelan Major League
   Baseball player

February 3
Blythe Danner, actress
Dennis Edwards, the Temptations

February 5
Nolan Bushnell, video game pioneer
Michael Mann, film director, writer, and
   producer
Craig Morton, football player

February 9
Joe Pesci, actor

February 23
Fred Biletnikoff, football player and coach

March 2
Peter Straub, author

March 9
Bobby Fischer, chess player
Charles Gibson, television journalist

March 16
Helen Armstrong, violinist

March 18
Kevin Dobson, actor
Dennis Linde, songwriter

March 20
Gerard Malanga, poet and photographer

March 22
Keith Relf, British rock musician

March 26
Bob Woodward, journalist

March 31
Christopher Walken, actor

April 3
Joey Vann, The Duprees

April 5
Max Gail, actor

April 11
Harley Race, professional wrestler

April 20
John Eliot Gardiner, English conductor
Edie Sedgwick, actress, socialite,
   model and heiress

April 24
Glen Dale, The Fortunes

April 28
John O. Creighton, astronaut

May 5
Michael Palin, British comedian

May 7
Rick West, The Tremeloes

May 13
Mary Wells, singer

May 24
Gary Burghoff, actor

May 25
Jessi Colter, singer and composer
Leslie Uggams, singer

May 27
Bruce Weitz, actor
Cilla Black, singer and entertainer

May 30
James Chaney, civil rights worker

June 15
Johnny Hallyday, French singer and actor

June 17
Newt Gingrich, politician
Barry Manilow, pop musician

June 23
James Levine, conductor

June 26
John Beasley, actor

June 27
Rico Petrocelli, baseball player

June 29
Maureen O'Brien, British actress

July 5
Curt Blefary, baseball player

July 20
Wendy Richard, British actress

July 23
Bob Hilton, game show announcer and host

July 25
Jim McCarty, British rock musician

August 10
Ronnie Spector, singer

August 15
Barbara Bouchet, actress

August 17
Robert De Niro, actor

August 19
Billy J. Kramer, singer

August 27
Tuesday Weld, actress

August 28
Lou Piniella, baseball player and manager
David Soul, singer and actor

August 30
Jean-Claude Killy, French skier

September 1
Don Stroud, actor

September 12
Maria Muldaur, singer

September 17
Gilbert Proesch, Italian-born artist

September 28
J.T. Walsh, actor

September 29
Lech Wałęsa, President of Poland, recipient of the Nobel Peace Prize

October 2
Franklin Rosemont, poet

October 6
Michael Durrell, actor

October 14
Lois Hamilton, model, actress and artist

October 22
Catherine Deneuve, actress

October 31
Paul Frampton, English physicist

November 4
Chuck Scarborough, news anchor

November 7
Joni Mitchell, Canadian musician
Dino Valente, musician

November 11
Doug Frost, Australian swimming coach

November 12
Wallace Shawn, actor

November 13
Jay Sigel, golfer

November 14
Peter Norton, software engineer and businessman

November 19
Aurelio Monteagudo, Cuban Major League Baseball player

November 21
Larry Mahan, rodeo cowboy

November 26
Marilynne Robinson, writer

December 8
Jim Morrison, rock musician

December 12
Grover Washington, Jr., saxophonist

December 15
Lucien den Arend, Dutch sculptor

December 18
Keith Richards, English rock guitarist and songwriter

December 21
Jack Nance, actor

December 23
Harry Shearer, actor and writer

December 31
John Denver, musician

Facts and Figures of 1943

President of the U.S.
Franklin Delano Roosevelt

Vice President of the U.S.
Henry A. Wallace

Population of the U. S.
136,739,353
Births
3,104,000

High School Graduates
Males: 55,865
Females: 69,998

Average Salary for full-time employee:
  $2,022.00
Minimum Wage (per hour): $0.30

© LIBRARY OF CONGRESS, PRINTS AND PHOTOGRAPHS DIVISION, CPH 3C17121

Average cost for:

Bread (lb.)	$0.09
Bacon (lb.)	$0.43
Butter (lb.)	$0.53
Eggs (doz.)	$0.57
Milk (gal.)	$0.62
Potatoes (10 lbs.)	$0.46
Coffee (lb.)	$0.30
Sugar (5 lb.)	$0.84
Gasoline (gal.)	$0.15
Movie Ticket	$0.29
Postage Stamp	$0.03
Car	$900.00
Single-Family home	$ 3,600.00

© 1943 SEPS

1943 TEXICO

Notable Inventions and Firsts

January 10: *The Better Half*, a quiz show, debuts on Mutual radio.

January 23: Duke Ellington plays at New York City's Carnegie Hall for the first time.

March 31: Rodgers and Hammerstein's *Oklahoma!* opens on Broadway. It becomes an instantaneous stage classic and goes on to be Broadway's longest-running musical up to that time—1948.

April 3: *The Billie Burke Show* airs on CBS Radio Saturday mornings.

May 17: The U.S. Army contracts with the University of Pennsylvania's Moore School to develop the computer ENIAC.

August 5: Women's Air Force Service Pilots (WASP) formed; consolidating the Women's Auxiliary Ferrying Squadron (WAFS) and Women's Flying Training Detachment (WFTD).

Sports Winners

NFL: Chicago Bears defeat Washington Redskins

World Series: New York Yankees defeat St. Louis Cardinals

Stanley Cup: Detroit Red Wings defeat Boston Bruins

The Masters: Not played due to World War II

PGA Championship: Not played due to World War II

October 30: The Merrie Melodies animated short film *Falling Hare*, one of the only shorts with Bugs Bunny getting out-smarted, is released in the U.S.

Frank Sinatra becomes a featured singer on *Your Hit Parade* radio program and co-star of the series *Broadway Bandbox*.

Hit song, "I've Heard that Song Before" performed by Harry James was no. 1 on the charts for 13 weeks.

The All-American Girls Professional Baseball League is founded by chewing gum mogul Philip K. Wrigley.

Live It Again 1943

Copyright © 2011 DRG, Berne, Indiana 46711

PROJECT EDITOR	Barb Sprunger
ART DIRECTOR	Brad Snow
COPYWRITERS	Jill Case, Jim Langham
EDITORIAL ASSISTANT	Stephanie Smith
PRODUCTION ARTIST SUPERVISOR	Erin Augsburger
PRODUCTION ARTIST	Erin Augsburger
COPY EDITORS	Emily Carter, Amanda Scheerer
PHOTOGRAPHY SUPERVISOR	Tammy Christian
NOSTALGIA EDITOR	Ken Tate
EDITORIAL DIRECTOR	Jeanne Stauffer
PUBLISHING SERVICES DIRECTOR	Brenda Gallmeyer

Printed in China
First Printing: 2011
Library of Congress Number: 2010904348
ISBN: 978-1-59217-305-1

Customer Service
LiveItAgain.com
(800) 829-5865

2 3 4 5 6 7 8 9